SIDEQUESTS

BRANDON ADAMSON

WASTELAND PRESS
www.wastelandpress.net

Wasteland Press
Shelbyville, KY USA
www.wastelandpress.net

SideQuests
by Brandon Adamson

First Printing – February 2008
ISBN: 978-1-60047-177-3

Printed in the USA

Dedicated to the old man in the cave

Part I
Beyond Redemption

"I'm seldom present in the present, you know.
Usually by the time I get to it, the present's passed
into the past."

–Wilfred Hyde-White as Dr. Goodfellow
"Buck Rogers in the 25th Century"

The Specter of Nostalgia for the Nostalgist, Nostalgic

Of course they do,
but I always seem to think that they don't think back,
outside the freshly opened Pandora's box within a box,
from within a box from within the one
we're boxed in.
Many people live life on the inside looking out or not.
Like a great actor in action, their presence exists in the present tense,
tending to events current, without the tensions or pretensions
of the self conscious.
They don't know what they'll never miss
The frivolity of their loyalties to their memories leads them,
leaves them room to move on.
They see no reason to hold on.
Caught up in the moment, in a moment, with it they
will soon be long gone.
But hold on!
There are those of us who live life on the outside looking in,
or looking back, looking forward to the past.
From afar, but still playing the part of participation,
viewing the whole preposterous celebration
as a mass grave, with one foot within.
Like a ghost performing the same routine,
repeatedly, unable to detach ourselves from an anxiety
over repeated histories, always remembering the endings
and their mournings, the mornings after.
Through memories and how they felt,
either by ourselves…
or viewed through the prism of the eyes of others
in texts, explicitly expressed through the lens
of their felt tipped pens.
Before it's over, a sadness over inevitably,
the future memories being amassed,
conscious already that they won't last.
Some of us become nostalgic for events before they even pass.
Missing things before they're even gone,
we long for and will soon become fond of
even the darkest days yet to come.

Embarking on a constant quest to reclaim the past,

the endless reminiscence, an infinite regress,
a paradox of recapturing the reclamation itself.
We resist and persist even amidst all forms of change,
for we never will, but wonder why things ever have to.
Always missing, though not quite missing out,
still taking our licks, while all the while
waxing nostalgic for nostalgia of being nostalgic for tomorrow
though not quite ready for it,
I am already for even this.

Beyond Redemption

"The Longest Road is the Road to Redemption", read the
caption of a car advertisement that caught my eye
as I was flipping through the pages of an airline magazine
while flying high at one of the low points in my life.
It really runs true.
Often times the road to redemption, with time and experience,
gets longer, lonelier, and more difficult to navigate
than it ever was in the beginning.
Like the cell of a little white lie that divides and multiplies,
the path back off the beaten,
leads to ever more and more complicated math.
While in the process of attempting to redeem yourself, you end up
creating seemingly even more reasons to redeem, as you make the next
  mistakes in trying to redeem yourself for past mistakes, and must then
  redeem yourself for failure to redeem yourself for failing to redeem
  yourself
for trying and failing miserably in the first place!
Make no mistake, it's
 like a mechanic who breaks something while trying to fix
something that he broke while trying to fix something
and so on, the road goes on and on,
until it's just a bridge too far and you feel like giving up
enough to make you dizzy, enough to make a man off and jump.
When you're beyond redemption,
it seems the only redemption is beyond.
From a first kiss to a lost cause,
you find yourself trapped,
caught in your own private episode of the twilight zone.
The story of redemption is the story that always works,
but hardly ever does.
The road to my own redemption
for failures and past mistakes
is indeed a long one, so wish for me safety in this unpleasant journey.
The veracity of a tenacity,
an ability to stubbornly persist and foolishly proceed
in the face of futility, but really,
absolving myself of all the guilt of the self absorbing,
amidst the broken bits of machinery
behold, an eye still gleaming,
perhaps the only redeeming quality(if any).

The Cards

What a card!
that bard must have been who said
"It's in the cards."
There's nothing in the cards
but card.

The Cards part II

"It was written."
So said the Arab to Lawrence of Arabia,
implying there was nothing that could be done,
no point in even attempting to save the young man
who had fallen off the camel, been separated from the caravan and
left for dead in the desert.
According to the Arab, the young man's fate had already been decided.
"Nothing is written!" was Lawrence's impassioned reply
in the famous scene where Peter O'Toole
gallantly races back into the desert and risks his own life to miraculously
  save the young man (who he ironically is forced to kill later in the film,
  thus in the Arabs' minds
re-affirming the original assertion that indeed "it was written") .

Fast forward fifty years from the release of "Lawrence of Arabia",
and everywhere you go you encounter people blabbering things like
"Maybe it just wasn't meant to be,"
"It just wasn't in the cards,"
"The lord works in mysterious ways," etc.
It's quite alarming that such ludicrous statements (if taken even remotely
  literally)
could be and in fact are being made by grown men and women!
In reality, there's nothing in the cards, and nothing is or isn't meant to
  be.
It's highly questionable whether the lord or some such deity even exists,
or ever existed for that matter, which is the only way one can logically
  assume
that such a beast "works in mysterious ways".
There's no evidence of it's very existence, mysterious indeed!
I'm sorry, but none of us are that important.
With all the billions of people on Earth,
all the planets in the solar system,

all the stars in the galaxy,
all the galaxies in the universe,
how could anyone be so arrogant,
so ignorant,
so mystically hubristic
enough to believe there are supernatural forces at play
that pertain to a single living individual,
that there are things meant specifically for them.
When it comes down to it,
we're all just peons in the grand scheme of things
of which there is no scheme in the grand,
no master plan.

What a card!
that bard must have been who said
"It wasn't in the cards."
There's nothing in the cards
but card.

A Plausible Deniability

Always reluctant to be one
to deny myself the ability
of deniability.
instead of a culprit
I can offer a caveat
give myself a way out
a safe place
by which to save face.
claim the foolishness
didn't really exist
a way to explain
on a distant day
how I didn't really mean
all the things I meant to say.

Remade in Their Image

Remakes for the most part are a disappointing phenomenon. Why do
people feel the need to remake classics, and redo masterpieces, thus
leaving our culture's sacred artistic ruins in ruin. Some are simply eager
to cash in on regurgitating old ideas, as the tried and true is a proven
moneymaker, and as the antithesis of artistic integrity and fond
memories, the market hates uncertainty. Others favor remakes as an
homage to the original work, but this is merely empty and ironically,
usually the end result tends instead to be rather insulting, missing
everything, including the meaning that may have made the original
groundbreaking, or interesting, something instrumental if not
monumental in leading to its succeeding. Support for remakes also
derives from people who claim that something, whether it be a video
game, a movie, a song, needs "updating" for the new generation, so that
they may appreciate it, believing the current crop of flat screen tweens
would not have the attention span, the patience or the capacity to accept
it in it's current antiquated state. In other words, it should be remade in
their image; fast pace, action packed, with concepts easily "graspable",
more controversial, superficial, and basically something that's able to
hold the attention of your average undereducated, uninterested text
messaging teenager.

Under the guise of remaking, people are in effect rewriting, even
obscuring history, as the new "appreciators" most often are not even
made aware, and may in fact never discover that a prior(superior)
version exists. Many of the things that are being remade for today's
society are in fact things which some of us nostalgically hold near and
dear as an illustration of everything that's wrong with (and as a form of
escapism from) today's society. Instead of teaching people how to
appreciate old things, how to increase their attention span, and how to
grasp the concept an original masterpiece was trying to convey, they
would rather make it more "accessible" to accommodate those who
could not appreciate it, would be unable to grasp it etc, thus discarding
much of the underlying theme which they thought made it such a great
idea to remake in the first place! It's like if someone said the Mona Lisa
should be redone, because it is too plain and young people would find it
boring or unattractive to look at. But would this be anything other than a
sad irony, a missing of the boat? Should something simply be remade
to accommodate the ignorant masses, or should people be forced to
learn to appreciate it if they are to deserve to?

Tomorrow, will people remake the remade films of today, in their own
image? so that they will be interesting to themselves?
Or wouldn't we prefer for them to understand us, the lessons we learned,
who we really were, what we believed, what we said, what we really
meant, in our own carefully chosen words?

The Easily Distracted

With each new rabbit's foot
and every magic trick in the book,
the potion of interest wears off quickly,
when tasked with such the arduous task
of keeping the youth of today entertained.
Even with the expanded wingspan of imagination,
and the magnetic charm of animal magnetism,
one finds it difficult to continuously attract
the attention span of the easily distracted.

I Remember it Like I was There

Like an old dog or an elephant never forgets,
remember,
someone with an excellent memory
and a tendency toward nostalgia
remembers everything.
Just by being attentive,
with an attention to-
they can recall the most minute details, places,
events, exact times…
Often time, they can even remember
the way things happened even better than the people
who were actually there.

Of Mice and Manticores

It's always a struggle to get to the core
of what's eating at the heart of the manticore
Who are we?
Why are we here and what does it mean?
another day, another dream.
That's merely the difference
between the mice and the manticores

those who are, or
at least from afar appear as worker bees,
who don't think to know,
don't look and just don't care to see.
Like the martians chronicled,
their secret of life is just to be.

Then there are,
the ones who differ
meaning those who prefer
to defer to dreams,
the manticores who would be queen
part men, part lions,
alert and aware
they must beware of the three blind mice
looking for the cat.
potentially, exponentially,
they are increasing everywhere.

In the future, as in the past,
like the spirit of the pioneers,
have such creatures all but disappeared?

Before The Fall

Take the fall,
the season when darkness falls earlier,
that makes me think of all the lonely falls
once spent falling asleep alone,
the pitiful perils and pitfalls
a result of previous falls fallen in life,
falls taken in the days before
my heart took the fall,
a trip from which if all else fails,
see you next.

The Present Tense

I do have a present in mind,
though it is not yet in hand, presently.
But when the time comes,
I will present it,
will have been presented

My Room

My room
a living room not a 'living room'
a red room
a blue room
a green room
a yellow room
a cream room
this room
another room
more room!
no room...
a dying room not a 'dining room'
a new room

The White Record Player

It's like the white record player
I had when I was a kid,
with those read-along records.
There were so many of them
one for every fairy tale,
for all the latest now dated movies.
I could keep myself occupied for hours
with that plastic, white record player.
Always a certain sound-
specific to each story-
when you heard it-
would signal
that it's time to turn the page…

Return Visitor

In the year 1993
looking into the mirror on the door
while showering,
I would make a plea
for at that moment
my future self
to visit me.
If indeed someday time travel would be possible.

And when I would not appear,
it was always a disappointment
to think that I might give up
and forget about all the things
I wanted to accomplish.

But here I am.
I have come back to that memory
fulfilling your dream.
revealing myself to my own
to show you things,
how they are
what they will mean,
and what you are to be.

What you do with this information,
will be my scientific discovery
upon my return.
If it precipitates what I anticipate
on a parallel line,
we may never know the difference.
More importantly,
what was/am I thinking?
The water's running.

CYOA

In a parallel universe, I could have been a tragic hero, or even a
mythological creature, perhaps a centaur or a manticore, rather I'm a
mere rumorwhore, a street urchin disguised as a boy emperor. I would
have made a great dictator, value loyalty over ability or do I have oh so
many enemies, seems like everyone's out to get me, but just like
"Invasion of The Body Snatchers", it's always scary when people
change, wake up one day you don't even recognize them,
it could even be your best friend, and we're now living in a world
controlled by pods, some might call it paranoia, that's the story of that's
the glory of love, and just like a choose your own adventure, there's so
many possible endings, unlike the past you can't escape, you change
your future when you change lanes. So maybe I'm a poor excuse for an
oligarchist, nostalgic for the old monarchists, my soul's at it's best when
it's at it's darkest, but did you know that every caesar has his brutus, like
even jesus had his judas, if he even exists, cause I don't believe in god
or any of that nonsense, It's all a lot of hocus pocus, still there's lessons
to be learned from it, after all it's metaphoric, and like the concept of
understated sarcasm, so few people actually grasp it. I've always been
partial to Greek myths. Granted, we could be sitting around and eating
pomegranate, in the lost city of Atlantis, instead pretty soon we'll all be
speaking Spanish, on the bright side, I like some girls who are
Hispasian, a mix of Asian and Hispanic, I guess that's just the human
side of it, Richard Nixon said it best, you in the press you couldn't be
interested in that, you're only interested in who shot John, everyone
wants a smoking gun, I just want to do what needs to be done, work
hard like to have a little fun, to dance is my deliverance, 11:11 wishes
are an ineffective tactic in romance.In a moment, one day my time is
going to come, after all this is Brandon's run, and just as I sing this so
called song, so my life clock's ticking on, one has such a small window
of opportunity, with which to change the future's history, and I'm
always still the same old me, but just like the man who folded himself,
there's so many different versions of us, when you're trying too hard not
to look like you're trying too hard without looking like you're trying too
hard not to look like you're trying too hard, it's all a big paradox. In the
theory of infinite regression, I'm just a boy taking a picture of myself
taking a picture of myself taking a picture of myself taking a picture of
myself taking a picture of myself. It's really quite difficult, moving
forward to the past, an endless relentless, futile, worthwhile? struggle to
get back to frame one, and with each and every brand new day, through
every face and time and place, the closer and further away it becomes.

The Hand is Pinker Than the Eye

Let me just say that I identify deeply with the pink panther
(cartoon version)
All he ever wants to do is just relax and enjoy himself, but
the world doesn't ever let him.
He's always going on these sort of "misadventures"
where everything goes wrong,
but still he just kind of stubbornly keeps at it even as
each and every new clever attempt to solve the situation backfires,
compounds itself, and ends up making it even worse.
That expression of futility that he gets on his face
when he turns toward the "camera" after a failure,
turns my TV screen into a mirror.

In particular there's the routine of repetition,
and the attempted repetition of the routine.
That's all the Pink Panther desires is to engage in
his simple pleasant activities, but the forces at play in the world,
tragically never allow it.
The Pink Panther always starts out with some
ordinary everyday project to improve his quality of life
ever so slightly, and then things start to go wrong
until it becomes a complete catastrophe and he eventually gives up
and the episode is over until the next and the cycle starts all over again.

Let me just say that I deeply identify with the pink panther…

Springtime in Paris

Looks to me like springtime in Paris...
suddenly, finally everything's perfect.
And I know that it's not real,
and it won't really last,
already looking like the past.
But still, it's the illusion
I prefer to reality.

Springtime in Paris with a twist..
springtime in Paris in Phoenix

Salad days are here at last!
It's all over, just as fast.
I'm looking forward to the past.

In a wine glass I see a reflection...
somewhere far off there's perfection.
It's true things aren't quite what they seem,
on the side where the grass is always green.
Even though, it's highly unlikely to be so...

(from here,)

that glass still looks half full.

Springtime in Paris with a twist..
springtime in Paris in Phoenix

Salad days are here at last!
It's all over, just as fast.
I'm looking forward to the past.

Can't seem to redeem that dream of redemption...
run away join the foreign legion.
Just a fool for Dien Bien Phu,
There's no beau geste left to gravitate to.

Anyhow I know it's just for pretend,
already know how that story ends,
'some men join to forget,
others to be forgotten'

Some people will do anything to be remembered.

No time but
for solitude and reflection.
I'm looking beyond redemption.

A creation of the schism
between illusion and reality
is the part that's the art
of the escape artist
in his place of escapism.

Springtime in Paris with a twist..
springtime in Paris in Phoenix

Here and There Then and Now and Then Again

here
and there,
then!
and now...

and then....?
again!

Part II
Despair to Spare

"Now that's a real shame when folks be throwin' away a
a perfectly good white boy like that." –Better Off Dead

Despair to Spare

Spare me, the inconsistency,
but more importantly,
don't, but leave me alone,
and spare yourself the grief.
Believe you me, if you need any,
I've got despair to spare,
more than you could shake a stick at!
Despair to spare,
from the fact which lends itself
to and from a tendency toward
train wrecks, turtlenecks,
and the more pressing matters of
the expressively depressed.
Highly sensitive to the intensity
of my own insensitivity and insecurity,
yet still photosensitive to those of a light-hearted nature.
Not very sympathetic,
just another pathetic poetic drivel spouting drivelet,
a striver with the drive
and desire to be nothing but a caricature,
merely the picture of a broken fixture of society.
Either way, remember to always look both ways,
I forget.
Like the chicken and the egg
which came first,
the sensitive poets or the stereotypical image of us
as such, grieving and pontificating away
at a 70's poetry reading,
preconceivedly meeting our expectations
halfway to the cliché?
So spare me, the inconsistency,
or more importantly,
have you been to Target lately and seen the constituency?
don't, but leave me alone and spare yourself the grief.
Believe you me, if you need any,
I've got despair to spare.
Like what's left of
what's vanished
in the thin air that remains with the ego of a deflated tire,
I've got despair to spare.

Despair For Men

'half the man you used to be'

As is often the origin of sources of despair itself, "Despair For Men" began with what seemed like a neat idea, when I was once told if there was a scent to describe me it would be "despair", making reference to a possible new cologne for men, not likely to be hitting the shelves any time soon.

Is despair for men right for you?

Despair For Men is recommended for any of the following people:

1. A cop who has been thrown off the force for accidentally shooting an unarmed teenager, and whose wife and children have left him, and has recently taken to the bottle.
2. The archetype romantic hero who doesn't get it or the girl even though he saw unrealistic, misleading movies that led him to think taking on said character would be effective in romantic pursuits.
3. A stock broker who has to go home and explain to his wife that they lost everything, who contemplates jumping out a window and plummeting to his undignified death, but is too cowardly to actually go through with it.
4. Someone who loses all his money in Las Vegas, and then ends up owing money to the loansharks who gave him more money to gamble with after he ran out.
5. One who is in a relationship with a "busy girl" who always makes time for everybody but him.
6. Any guy who suspects his girlfriend may be cheating on him,
  or wanting to or even whimsically daydreaming about cheating on him.
7. Guys with suicide fantasies and daydreams about how cool it would be etc.
8. Straight males who live in predominantly gay areas and are constantly harassed by gay men, as well as gay men who live in predominantly straight neighborhoods and are constantly harassed by straight women or just plain dickheads.
9. Men who are hypochondriacs and always think they are sick, or who are hypochondriacs but also actually are indeed ill, even more so than they had ever imagined.
10. One who constantly refers to himself as "a shell of a man".

11. Guys who are poor and starving to death, which is never particularly pleasant except to boast about later when you are no longer.
12. Anyone who was laid off from any job, anytime for any reason, legitimate or otherwise, especially from dot com companies.

So, now I know some of you are dying to purchase this stuff so you can put out the scent and plant your seed in some girl who feels sorry for you, or is tricked into thinking you're half the man you once were thanks to the camouflaging abilities despair for men will have to give the appearance of a more superficial personality. Enjoy!

Despair (for men)$15.00

The Great Plains

I'll take mine plain-
plain jane
plain clothes
what's that?
you're eating it plain?
how I love...
the great plains
turn my heart into a flood plain
of pain,
the plain...the plain!

High Card

Bet your max if you want to win!
but
never bet your max unless
you're prepared to lose everything
more than once
I gambled everything on one girl and lost.
Now, like the cat who's been
thrown in the bathtub too many times,
I'm embittered for life.

A Bard Out of Time

A spoony bard,
barred within the prison of his own time.
In his future, left behind
bars, displaced in a time and place,
relegated to a century, a decade, a day,
anytime and everywhere he doesn't belong.

Confounded by the signs of the times,
caught somewhere in the confines of a civilization in decline.
Bewildered by the wilderness of the lost woods
where once stood Sherwood Forest.

With what little precious time is left,
finds findings in rhymes, and nostalgia reflects.
A sadness at all he would have liked to accomplish,
no longer the power to bend the line,
he knows, he's a bard out of time.
Overflowing with jovial personality, maybe,
but polyunsaturated with the melancholy
of knowing the time remaining in the glass
is finally empty.

He begins to envision himself,
as he exists in others' memories
not notably remembered for anything but being
a bard out of time

Beautiful Dreamer

The water's only skin deep.
We could live forever in an underwater city,
beneath all the human debris.
In all irony, despite the hubris,
humility in reality is truly my only quality if any.
When it comes to romance,
like Klondike Kat, I'm up a tree.
Or maybe I'm just a lonely, longing for a clonely
other version of myself in someone else,
a hologram even.
I'd settle for anyone remotely,
who even likes me?
It's a damn tragedy. Behold, the eye in beauty,
a mirror version of me who can see through the calamity of errors,
the narcissist's hurt vanity,
and bam!
Like the towers it's twinsanity,
terror on the high seas,
as far as I can see beyond the pillars of Hercules.
An overactive imagination,
not worthy of a ship captain,
megalomania of a chieftain,
more in common with a James Bond villain.
Always tend to lose in the end,
if at first you don't succeed,
try, try again.
Whatever happened to Mordred and Morgana
and everything that's interesting about Camelot?
I've got a good voice and a lot to say,
but then I can't really sing.
Lucky for me, and fun as it may seem,
all men are great in their dreams.

A Love Affair With Humidity

I can't remember the exact moment
I fell in love with humidity,
it just sorta happened
a few years back
I began to see her in a different light
no longer a threat
and more than just a friend
a moisturizer
a preservative
an anti-inflammatory agent
humidity as the underdog
the unappreciated
and thus my love affair with humidity began
I wish we could be together all the time

A Narrow Escape

a breakup is like a narrow escape
the more tragic the loss
the more better off
the narrower the
the escape
from marriage
children
the ordinary simple life
and death.
a passionate love affair
is one thing
settling down
is always settling
for a life less interesting
search and avoid love
because
one false move
one false beat of the heart
and you're back safely on nature's assembly line

After All

After all,
the things we've gone through
always seem silly
after all is said and done
no, not right now
while we're young
after all
maybe the entry
isn't in the diary of tomorrow
the end all be all
after all

Drawing, Bored

I'm so bored
nothing to do
there's nobody on the phone to talk to
nobody I want, too.
Any plain girl with in a scarf in her hair
anyone will do.
I'm so bored
it's back to the drawing,
bored

Bag of Bags

what's in the bag?
a bag
within a bag
within a bag
it's a bag of bags
a bag to end all bags
a grab bag
a handbag
a ho bag
it's in the bag!
of bags

Chain Letters Never Sent

It's all those chain letters
I never sent
that I only read
without passing them
to five internet friends

I never gave anything back
of all I received.
In return that's what I get
and I owe all my bad luck to them

So when the next one comes
I might just hit send
might just forward them
because I like my friend
and I need all the help I can get

Choose Your Own

Life is like
a choose your own adventure book
you keep re-reading
until you get the ending
you want
constantly in denial
and always skipping ahead
continuing on
as if the bad endings never happened

Compliments of

Elementary my dear (but not Watson)
but rather in this case it's complimentary,
at least it was meant to be,
and by meant I mean it was intended,
as opposed to predetermined.
In any case,
a well placed compliment
can serve as the condiment,
the breath mint
for a new relationship.

It can act as the first scent,
can make the dent
in someone's defenses
thaw their senses
a well placed compliment
will get your foot in the door
only so far

while a misfire can backfire
and set you back even further
down more toward the ground floor

Costume Drama

Very well I contradict myself
knock myself out
looking for a knockout,
won't settle for a knockoff.
A friendship bracelet
is never enough.

Alone in a department store
I forgot what I came here for…
Thank you, I'm just browsing for
maybe I need your designer love.

Very well I can distract myself
psyche myself out
in time I've learned to live without,
shielded by material things
immortal while we're shopping

Alone in a department store
I forgot what I came here for…
Thank you, I'm just browsing for
maybe I need your designer love.

Very well I'm lying to myself
what's it really all about?
just browsing, daydreaming
ambiance is everything.

A sidequest for designer drugs
left our clothes covered in blood.
A sidequest for designer love
became a costume drama.

Erotic Thriller

A character
rugged handsome
messy apartment
down on his luck
wife and kids have left him or been killed
thrown off the force
and has taken to the bottle
meets attractive mysterious woman
a debutante
adds excitement
danger
empty wine glasses
saxophone music
giant piece of abstract art on the wall
cut to softcore
dead body
murder
betrayal
double cross
triple cross
multiple plot twists
violent climax
ambiguous ending

Five Times

Let the phone ring five times
hang up
no more, no less
any more they're too busy to talk to you
anyhow
they're not anxious to.
anything less is a waste of nerve
or just plain creepy
never leave a message
or you're only cheating yourself
leaving yourself
no reason to call back again

Fountain Drink of Youth

a thirst
empty cup
filled with ice
pour beverage
commence consumption
the first sip
drink more
the glass half full
almost gone
the chewing of ice
empty cup...

Wallowing in Obscurity

It's to be expected,
that which normally one wouldn't be expecting
to expect.

I've never been one to speak pejorative,
Rather, always the penchant for mentioning the perception
through an obscure reference.
Like a secret code, which if recognized will bode well
for a bond of comradery,
a rapport established instantly
with those wallowing in obscurities,
or with the hope to,
but often the failure of an incubus
to ignite the initiation of imaginations,
but not curiously, even the mere curiosity,
(disappointingly, predictably, mostly)
of the incurably incurious,
disinterested parties.

There's Always One

There's always one, in every group.
In every group there's always,
always one who doesn't belong,
the one who drifts from group to group
and never quite belongs.
There's always one who's there to say so.
He knows you're not one of us,
not one of us.

Every time you join a group,
it's never for too long.
I've got a friend in every group.
That's all you need is one.

I get your drift, so if you drift
from group to group like I do,
I'm here to say, that you can stay.
You can say you're one of us.
You're one of us.
And it's okay,
There's always one!

Orange You Glad

Did you get me an orange?
    Yes, and I made sure to get you the best one.
Do you even know how to pick out oranges?
    Why yes of course. I got you the orangest orange.

Just Saying

Understand,
what I said before,
I'll just say again.
I know just what you mean,
when you're saying things,
you don't really mean.

It's all right.
It was only a dream.
It's hardly worth mentioning,
all of this,
everything,
doesn't mean a thing,
I'm just saying.
Look, I'm just saying.

Understand,
what I said before,
I'll just say again,
and so it would seem
all of this
everything,
doesn't mean a thing,
I'm just saying.
Look. I'm just saying.

Acceptance is the Cure

I just want someone to accept me
for who I am
 "But you don't even accept yourself
  for who you are!"
I accept myself for being someone
who can't accept who they are.
So I guess I'm looking for an exception,
someone who accepts me for being someone
who accepts themselves for being someone
who can't accept who they are.

Silver Lining For a Heart of Gold

No matter how many millions
the pieces that remain
of a shattered heart,
swiftly the dreams dashed,
gray the skies ahead,
long the odds,
bleak the outlook,
deep and dark the depression,
heavy a burden,
nothing your everything...

a silver lining for a heart of gold,
no matter how miserable your life has become,
you're always just one look away
from love at first sight

Overwhelming

Understanding begins
as sadness overwhelms
when love underwhelms
but if it doesn't,
if acceptance comes
when a socialite
ends their social life
death might as well
whelm
for all intents and purposes

The Hamster's Predicament

Have you ever heard of the hedgehog's dilemma? They discuss it in the Evangelion anime series(it is the title of one of the episodes), but the concept is thought to have originated from a German philosopher, Arthur Schopenhauer, but which Freud introduced into psychology as an analogy for human relationships.

"Hedgehog's Dilemma" refers to the idea that the closer two beings become, the more vulnerable they are to being hurt by one another. Paradoxically, if they remain far apart, they will each feel the pain of loneliness. This stems from the fact that hedgehogs have sharp spines and will hurt each other if they get too close.

Though mostly unrelated, the concept of the hedgehog's dilemma, led to an observation which I call "The Hamster's Predicament"
(which has undoubtedly been observed by others and is probably already called something else by someone somewhere) and how it relates to modern relationships.

I recall hearing about in science, that if you take any two hamsters, a male and a female and put them in a cage together, they'll mate(big surprise). However, when you take away the male hamster, and replace it with a new male hamster in the cage, the female will actually destroy the fetus and proceed to mate with the new male!

The same thing likely applies to humans, and they don't even realize it. That's why long distance relationships never work, because if the two people are not together, the female will consciously or unconsciously seek another mate at some point as a means of security and survival.

Now the male may find another mate as well, but it's different in his case, because that's his job. He's supposed to try and mate with as many females as possible in his lifetime anyway. It's only those "intelligent rats" with the sophistication and self discipline to remain loyal, who resist this behavior, for they have become conscious and (slightly) more self-aware of who and what they are than the average bear.

Having stated the bad news, the good news is that some previously thought long distance relationships can now work! Thanks to modern technology like cellular phones(free long distance, phone cards etc) email, frequent flier miles, text messaging,… you can really go all out if both parties are determined. At the same time, if technological advancements reduce the proverbial "distance" both actually and metaphorically, can long distance relationships really still be categorized as such?

In fact long distance relationships really still don't work, but rather in actuality the distance has merely been reduced to a manageable point that nature finds biologically acceptable. In other words, long distance relationships can be successful only by eliminating or shortening the distance!

The hamster's predicament can also manifest itself on a smaller scale, that need not cross state, continental, or intergalactic lines.
Like if you work different schedules, or your girlfriend goes to school, and starts to spend time with other guys in other seemingly non-romantic aspects of life, she will inevitably develop interest in them regardless of how subjectively ugly or otherwise unappealing they would be amongst your average gaggle of men. In the olden days, wives just stayed at home all day, and spent the vast majority of time with their husbands, so the hamster's predicament was much less of an issue in everyday life. Except of course in the case of husbands/boyfriends going off to war and often having to receive painful letters in the field or nasty surprises upon returning home, such as returning from a lengthy campaign in the pacific to their wives suddenly well versed and immersed in some perplexing pregnancy term mathematics.

But nowadays, where you have people always traveling, working late with their boss, going to school, having opposite schedules, etc they are basically putting themselves in dozens of circumstances or situations where they won't be together, and it's only a matter of time before disaster strikes and ladies night out becomes girls gone wild.

Think of it this way, it's like how when you work somewhere or you're bored in class, and there aren't really any cute girls, so you start to develop a crush on the only "remotely attractive girl", or in some even less gender numerically advantageous situations, the only girl. Or worse?

Nobody is perfect though, maybe not even humans in their predictability. I haven't figured out a way to successfully defy nature and triumphantly overcome the hamster's predicament, but I have learned the hard way to be mindful of the distance between us so as to avoid falling into it.

Sea Creatures

*"Soon all the beasts of the world will be transformed
into one giant creature"*- The Mana Tree, Secret of Mana

Remember where the seeds used to be
trees used to be
she used to be
right over there.
Once I loved a sea creature
now I just see creatures
see creatures
everywhere

Do you remember where the seeds used to be
reeds and even weeds used to be
we used to be
right over there.

Try to remember where the seeds used to be
trees used to be
she used to be
right over there.
Once I loved a sea creature
now I just see creatures
see creatures
see?
creatures.
Everywhere…

The Creeps

Quite often times
people who say you're really creepy
quite often
come to find themselves
cavorting with the real creeps

The Secret of Unsuccess

If someone fails to succeed
in their own time
whether it be in love,
art,
music,
or life in general
then the best they can hope for
is to be remembered fondly
as someone who
was unappreciated in their own time
by their own kind
in a future line.

Human Side

People are just objects
for pleasure
and amusement,
to be used, exploited
for personal gain
realpolitik among friends
people are just things
merely creatures of convenience
to be callously disregarded
thrown away
people are just people,
until you visit their house
see pictures of them as children
family photographs,
loved ones,
and suddenly
what was once a people
is now a person,
someone else
now yourself,
human.

Leprosy

Quick look in the mirror
take a picture
destroy it immediately
it's what I see
two out of every three
I can cure it
only temporarily.
Leprosy,
it's what always happens to me.
It's just something I have to deal with.

The Nine of Lives

The first is always the first
the second is a bad remake
oxymoronic
the third isn't always the charm
the fourth can't be claimed as a dependent
the fifth is always being recreated
the sixth is the address to the beach
the seventh is not as bright as Arcturus
the eighth is never enough
the ninth is just no

To Get or Not to Get or

It's been said that
there are two types of people
those who get it
and those who don't.
But there are also those who,
while they themselves don't get it,
still recognize there's something
to be gotten
by someone,
somewhere.

The Meaning of All This

I mean,
I know I'm mean
sometimes
but you know
I mean…
I mean well
if you know what I mean

Who Cares

I don't care
he doesn't care
about you
she doesn't care about me
are you listening
do you even care?
see nobody cares
like I care
if anyone cares

Who Knows

I know
like,
I don't know....
you know?
it's cool.

Workout Plan

Some girls are all about
wishing things would've worked out
or wondering why
things didn't work out
don't work out
won't work out
or if only this
or that
then things would've worked out.
It's as if instead of working things out
and things working out
all they really wanted was a good workout
I guess just let them
work themselves out
cause I just want things to work out
if that's cool

Amidst a Misogynist

*"Young woman, either you have been raised in some incredibly rustic
community where good manners are unknown or you suffer from the
common feminine delusion that the mere fact of being a woman exempts
you from the rules of civilized conduct."*
-Clifton Webb as Waldo Lydecker in "Laura"(1944)

In the thick of the mix
of the blitz of awe and beauty of beauties,
we have it would seem
a misogynist amidst.
Every red blooded man has one,
somewhere, perhaps within reason
and his ability to do so...

a sense of hopelessness
tendency toward bitterness
over the missed and the communications landing amiss,

something arising from the self conscious disdain of the self controlled
for those of the emotions uncontrolled,
the battle of the poised versus the noise for the sake of,
locked in a semi-permanent struggle with one another
are the mild temperament and the child temper.

Out on the town,
in the thick of the mix,
underlies this,
the misogynist amidst,
reluctant to relinquish the quest for the kiss
with the potential to vanquish the anguish
so prevalent
amidst the misogynist.

Bright Colors That Fade

To dream of the same,
night upon night,
an unfulfilled promise,
a loose end,
fit to be tied
like a noose around the neck..

Bright colors that fade,
wishing yours would stay,
kelly green into gray,
they'll just fade away
see the bright colors that fade
and the ones who stay
in the cycle that spins,
relentless.

but the spell...it wears off
and the dreams subside...
cured with precious time
a calmness at last,
becomes emptiness at best,
then nostalgia for nightmares,
of something new,
longing for their return,
with a vengeance they do…

but for a moment...alas!
bright colors at last.

and the cold heart it takes
the gold heart...
it breaks!
see the bright colors that fade
and the ones who stay
in the cycle that spins,
relentless

A Sleep

I'm asleep
Who cares if I miss sleep
because of you? not me.
I'm not really asleep
I can't really sleep when you're here
but I really can't sleep
when you're not here
I wish we couldn't really sleep together
every night
because then you would always
be here.

We'll Ride the Wind

The wind can be quite
when it's windy enough to be annoying
while not quite so windy that it's exciting
like a martian dust storm would be.

The wind, lightly,
rather than awe inspiring
becomes merely,
mildly irritating.
it messes up combovers
amplifies conversation,
and chaps the skin.
For some,
there's no happy medium
when it comes to quiet
and the wind.

Revivify

Your emotions,
your dreams, your wants and needs.
Your youthful energy!
I know what you're thinking
I don't know actually, but I know exactly
you think
I think
it's silly,
and that I'm rolling my eyes
about to insult you
with barely a sigh
and I am, but
so what!
in the grand scheme of things.
For really inside
I'm dying,
an at times living seems
listless and lifeless,
fruitless,
my oxygen is useless.
and you're the only thing
breathing life back into me.

On the Moon

On your mark!
on the move,
we could be on the moon
imagination
a rocket ship can take us there.

On the moon
both too cold and too warm
so we've been told
but inside,
the sadness, the music
beckons us.

So now we're on the move.
I'd rather be,
when we could be on the moon.
What's in the moon?
the moon pearl
the moon crystals.
us,
on the moon.
It's beautiful.

I Will Be With You Always

One time at a vintage clothing store
I purchased a jean jacket which
someone had handwritten something on the back,
in pink and white lettering,
"Je serai avec vous toujours" which
translates to "I will be with you always" in French.
It made me kind of sad as I guess they must have broken up,
and he had not even been too broken up about it
if he was willing to sell the garment off cheap to a used clothing store.
I probably would have kept it as one of my most prized possessions.

A few years later,
I came across the match,
meaning what must have been the female counterpart jacket
with the same inscription on the back.
I though it was interesting,
that she hung onto it for so much longer,
like maybe she had a harder
time letting go.

Or maybe I'm reading way too much into it,
and they just moved on and
needed some cash so they sold the jackets.
And I wasn't even there, yet here I am,
probably the only one who still cares.
It will be with me always, but really.

Appeasement

I'm always experimenting
with whether it's feasible
to conceive the inconceivable,
to appease the apparently unappeasable.
I try,
and manipulate and maneuver and
never quite get anywhere,
but somehow still manage to buy
myself some time with which to
not get there.

Compatibility

I've given the best of my ability,
but it would seem compatibility with another
person is paradoxically beyond the realm
of possibilities for me.

  "I just don't know how I feel about this anymore"
   "It just doesn't seem to be working out"

Well if you're not interested in me romantically
anymore, don't like me
and no longer wish to date me...

  "It's not that. I really like you a lot.
   I just don't think we're compatible"

Right. So you don't like me enough
for it to supercede and overcome
the ways in which we are incompatible,
which aren't many.
I guess I just need someone who will
like me despite my incompatibility,
the way that I would them, but then again
I would be compatible with that person!
Will someone just please love me despite
our inability to achieve compatibility,
before I lose the ability?

Two Different Too Different

I beg to differ.
We're two different people, too different,
who cannot reconcile our irreconcilable differences
with one another.
Too different, the differences,
the distance between too far,
the stack too wide, piled too high to be set aside,
an elephant in the room
with no room left to negotiate.

Unlike the likeness of the alike,
we're similar only in that we've similarly
been voluntarily evicted,
convicted by our own convictions,
from point A to point B,
there's no letter in between.
Both would gladly pay the penalty
to believe their beliefs.

Some people are just too different.
Two different, same difference.
Others except or accept.
They persevere to preserve it,
the two different, not too different.

The Essence of Fluorescents

Try to capture
the essence
the metaphorical scent
of phosphorescence
in the fluorescents,
despite their fueling
the need for antidepressants
and a future scarce of descendants
of the once abundant,
soon to be extinct incandescents

for these things,
the fluorescents,
even in their inanimate
show us our life in a different light,
as it is, not as we wish.
and the pale green acts as
the painful shock,
we sometimes need to change it.

Carefully Chosen Words

Feel free
about your feelings
to ramble to your heart's content
if it is even possible
or even seems a cause worthy
who knows if that vessel is still sea worthy
to reach such a destination.
(I should hope not!)
but for me
when it comes to you
maybe!
It's one I have already reached.
My response,
though I may seem unresponsive
and may not do so
very promptly
or with what you perceive
an equal sense of urgency,
rest assured
I'm still listening.
In some ways we're all just too different
an abstraction, a distraction that's merely
a refracted fraction of my romantic interest,
for purely as romantics
we're clearly equivalent.
whereas you're feeling everything
and thinking, thinking,
just substitute foolish daydreaming
and inductive reasoning
again and again
there you have me,
a lifetime member,
of the remembering
if you will,
remember me.
You're just being,
a human being,
and I can be cold and calculating
like a machine,
sometimes I wonder if I even need oxygen to breathe.

Mechanically speaking,
the familiarity of unreliability
is all too familiar for me.

If there's a moment of silence
consider this
an indication of your identity
as someone who's worth
waiting for those
carefully chosen words
the ones I save for
the carelessly woven verse
meant for those who make me think first.
After all this I'm often wrong
sometimes
though my golden arrow aimed
heart and vision same
near perfect
when I don't see you
I just miss.
So we'll see.

Part III
Sidequests Aside

"…or evermore will be nevermore, forevermore."
-Secret of Evermore SNES

Sidequests

a day at the zoo, a first kiss, a lost cause, a premonition, a treehouse, abstract art, alchemy, all for nothing, all or nothing, alternate endings, ambiguity, and then some, andy warhol, angels, angst, anorexia, antiquers, ascii artwork, as it was, as you wish, atheism, audiobooks, baby blue, bad news bears, baja fresh, baths, being number one, being reasonable, being secretive, beyond escape, bellerophon, bionic implants, buck rogers, boca burgers, boring girls, bubblenomics, buying it back, buying time, cars all around, cassettes, castling, cavedwellers, centaurs, centurions, chainletters, chieftains, choose your own adventures, chrono trigger, cinderella, clingy girls, clothes, cohorts, contrarians, costume dramas, crash diets, dance moves, daydreaming, deductive reasoning, degree mills, diet coke, diet coke plus sucks, diet pepsi, doppelgangers, dorky girls, dracula, drama queens, dumb young girls, dutch constructivists, dvds, early nineties, eating, elegancy, ellsworth kelly, escapism, espers, exile, f scott fitzgerald, fairy tales, far away times, fascism, fighting with girls, film noir, flowers, fountain drinks, french foreign legion, general leo, general urko, getting there, gihugic, girls on the rebound, giving dirty looks, Gliese 581c, good manners, gossip, greek mythology, guest lists, happy endings, hating girls, holden caulfield, holding hands, hollow earth theory, hollywood, howard hughes, humidity, humility, hush money, infinite regression, illusion of gaia, inductive reasoning, intelligent design, james bond, jewel thieves, john dall, kelly green, kewliez, kid chameleon, kid icarus, kissing, kthxbye, lavender, link to the past, list art, listening to the same cd over and over, los angeles, lost andjealous, lost woods, lounging around, love, love affairs, loyalty over ability, lying a lot, made in the shade, madeupwordery, make out sessions, manticores, market research, masochism, meds, megalomania, mediocrity, memories, microwave popcorn, minimalism, misogyny, mod, mondo mod, monarchies, money, more time, moving day, my ex-girlfriend, my girlfriend, my room, mythological creatures, naptime, narcissists, nice girls, nintendo music, nostalgia, not dying, not getting vd, not new york, not sluts, not the 80's, now and then, obscure references, obsessive love, oligarchy, omfg, one gillion, optimism, otto preminger, overdoing it, oxymorons, pacing, pale people, paradoxes, partners in crime, partners in time, pastels, pegasus, perfect girls, pillpoppers, pillpopping, pills, pink panther cartoons, plaid, plain girls, planet of the apes, playing against type, polaroids, pool parties, pop music, pretty eyes, pretty things, quiet time, reasonable people, redeeming qualities, redundancy, repetition, return to the planet of the apes, rolling my eyes, romance, rothko, routine, rydia, sacrifice,

sad endings, satyrs, salvation, sea creatures, secret of evermore, secret of
mana, self-fulfilling prophecies, selling my soul, shapes, shy girls,
sidequests, singing, socially awkward girls, solitude, something weird,
springtime in paris, stepford wives, sundays, super nintendo, talking on
the phone, tempe, tennis, the 50's, the 60's, the 70's, the butterfly effect,
the concorde, the feudal system, the god of poverty, the glass half full,
the golden fleece, the grass roots, the pure of heart, the roman empire,
the turtles, the zombies, then and now, this side of paradise, the sword in
the stone, three wishes, time, time travel, tragic heroes, train wrecks,
turtlenecks, twee pop, two person bike riding, two words put together,
understanding, understated sarcasm, unicorns, vegenaise, vivacious
teenage girls, when things were great, whit stillman, wind, wine, your ex-
girlfriend, zardoz, zeal, zest for life, zeus, zoos, zzz...

Ship up or Shape out

Whether or not by myself
or a shaper,
somehow my mind was shaped
in such a way
to believe it's worth trying
to shapen the shape of shapes
we can only see
the way they're shaping up to be

"Side" Quests

Circle

So easy to be encircled
within the circle of friends
when you travel in the same social circles
of friends
caught up in a lie
that never begins
and never really ends
things easier said than done
come back around
to haunt you
to taunt you
surround you
in the circle
of friends
caught up in a lie
that never begins
and never really ends
until you seek out a new
social circle
going in circles
(it's a vicious circle)
encircled by friends

Square

You're nothing but a squire
if you're an equal side in the square.
equality equals normality and banality
and you'll never get anywhere in the square.
it's a bad neighborhood
for those seeking knighthood.
savoir-faire is everywhere
except the square,
where there's nothing even remotely interesting
in those four corners,
only squires squared.

Triangle

out of
love draws the triangle
the shape of things to come
3D
three sides to every story
a three way tie
a three way
the Bermuda triangle
the love triangle draws

Rectangle

Easy to get oneself tangled
in the rectangle
four corners
in which to be cornered
two large sides
two small
the left side
the right side
the winning side
the losing side
their side
my side,
which side of the rectangle
are you on?

Pentagon

All this pent up frustration
I command you!
be gone!
banish you to the 5th dimension
for me,
for us
it would be.
if only I were a magus,
or of my mind, a king

All this pent up frustration
I command you!
please be gone!

such are the cries heard from
within the walls of a pentagon

Hexagon

She puts the hex on you
and then she's gone.
such is life for the fledging young misogynist
caught within the confines
of the six, six, six!
sides of the hexagon.
surrounded,
confounded,
dumbfounded.
ultimately his concerns are well founded.
as they have been documented
throughout history,
romantically
his feet will remain grounded
until further notice.

Heptagon

Are you hip to the heptagon?
If so, what took you so long?
It's fab just like the hexagon,
but slightly more of a fad,
with sides seven fold,
it goes from hip to gone.

Better hop along, hop to it
and get hip to the heptagon
while it's still on. They just don't get
it's going once, going twice,
sold to and by the man,
always the highest bidder,
the movie ruiner,
who takes a small thing from the fringe
and brings it out to the open range
where the masses assemble,
line up to take aim in the process
destroying everything of meaning
and driving it back to the brink of extinction.
Those of the origin, long gone,
and the hip hop along
for they have already moved on,
to their new heptagon,
and didn't even stay long enough to witness
the sadness of those who stayed on.

Octagon

A brisk October walk at the fair,
"Halt! Who goes there?"
"Stop, in the name of the octagon!"
the world that's a circle gone phenomenally,
diagonally, rigidly wrong.
These days one cannot go anywhere,
or do anything without taking anything
from some form taking shape,
acting as an authority figure,
(whether legitimate or a nuisance vigilant)
putting an end to innocent fun and games
everywhere.

Nonagon

No way Jose.
Whether as the Germans say "nine"
or the French,
"non."
The answer is still no.
It's something of a recurring phenomenon
in the nonagon.
Like life on Melrose,
everybody always says no.
That idea is just a non starter in the nonagon
a place filled with such where none have gone.
You're just now starting to catch on
what goes on,
the struggle to exist for the optimist
who persists in the quiet quest
for a simple yes.

Those who against their will,
chose to remain anonymous
in their nonexistence,
are even still plotting their escape
from the cold, desolate
dungeon of the nonagon.

Decagon

Another decade
has come and gone in the decagon.
for me not much has changed
while others it seems
once deemed too young
have all but passed me in age.
They have children who play
while they themselves fully grown
beyond their wildest dreams
forgotten
replaced by more than mortgages
and more to pay.
If that is what it all means
to be a real man
or merely realistic,
then consider me
not really real,
a mystic, a mythically
mythic,
sick and incurable
with peter pan syndrome
but it's much more appealing
than becoming one of those
coming and going in droves.

Oval

A soul gives it sole
purpose
and is received by all
and rendered null
the standing ovation
is on vacation
in the oval,
sometimes an office

Sphere

Try to imagine the image
with the sheer magnitude
as seen from within the womb
beyond the atmosphere
through the magnetosphere,
the force field
which deflects and
protects us
on the sphere.
There's nothing to fear
but what's out there?
beyond the moon.
Some of us believe
other worlds
where other mere mortals see
merely spheres!

Trapezoid

Unable to avoid
the void
when one's falling into the trap
that's the trapezoid.
like a black hole nothing escapes
not much anyways
at one time or another
leaving behind a void
where once was something
a broken boy,
forever trapped in the trapezoid.

Parallelogram

There's no time like plenty of quiet time,
a soliloquy for the boy
and girl
carrying the telegram like a torch
in the parallelogram,
a parallel universe,
two dimensional,
with just one verse,
off somewhere
bearing right on course
traveling on identical directional paths
that never intersect
except with the exact
opposite.

Pixels and Polygons

To some, pixels will always be preferable to polygons.
Imaginative storylines will always be superior
to overblown spectaclactic cliches
and so called "awesome graphics".
Catchy and simple, thought provoking music
which promotes the lost virtues of quiet and solitude,
will be preferred over above ground blaring surround sound.
They will remain forever frozen in elation
at the prospect of the pixelation.
Others see no reason to resist
the temptation of the polyunsaturated
nature of the polygon.

Cylinder

Cylinder is the engine that propels man
to the outer reaches of his time and space,
and yet still,
the colander that strains and pains us all,
as always,
it's hard to decide what to throw away,
as almost always the linger of doubt over the decision
forever remains.
If only we could relegate the cynical to the cylindrical,
then we would surely be able to, that is
if anyone of us would be left to go
since there are the best of both enclosed
in the time capsule.

Cube

More than just a game
or a puzzle, but puzzling to solve
and escape just the same,
this block of ice,
the place where days, often years, cubed,
are time spent in place
wasted away in this meager space,
far from gleaming.

Pyramid

The "id" in the pyramid
is representative of the idiot in all of us,
so curiously suspicious
of what we should be in awe of.

*"There are those who believe that life here began out there, far across
the universe, with tribes of humans who may have been the forefathers of
the Egyptians, or the Toltecs, or the Mayans. That they may have been
the architects of the great pyramids, or the lost civilizations of Lemuria
or Atlantis. Some believe that there may yet be brothers of man who even
now fight to survive..."*

–so states the narrative at the beginning of Battlestar Galactica

And thus leads us to the Egyptians and the origins of the pyramids,
Which despite claims made by those,
and no concrete evidence to the contrary of what follows,
were built by and are entirely human.

However, like many empty hypotheses derived
from overactive imaginations, and faulty reasoning,
it does make you think, how
5,000 years in the past, there may have already
existed and became extinct, civilizations out there in the universe
millions of years more advanced than us as we are today.

Did we evolve from something, a primordial highly complex pack of
sea monkeys, intentionally dispersed and created in something the
equivalent of
a cosmic petri dish?
merely some highly intelligent creature's
B- science experiment?

There is no scientific evidence of this, but what if?!

Thus, the origin of the pyramids, entirely human,
piques the curiosity, which leads to the examination,
and perhaps eventual discovery(or not)
of broader more interesting things.

If nothing else, the pyramid was the basis of
one of the greatest 1970's game shows of all time, and
the pyramids themselves were featured in a terrific
sequence between Roger Moore and Jaws
in the James Bond film "The Spy Who loved Me."

The "id" in the pyramid
is representative of the idiot in all of us,
so curiously suspicious
of what we should be in awe of.

Rectangular Prism

Thinking outside the box,
coloring outside the proverbial lines,
the boundaries of thought,
like the game "Operation,"
will give you a shock,
get you caught in
the prison of the rectangular prism.
four walls, but not squared
"away with you!" "off with him!"
as you go.
an imperfect system
when viewed through the prism,
this prison of the rectangular kind.

Rhombus

Stealing from only those who would rob or have robbed us,
in order to avoid a bust, watch
a thief among us,
that's me
like monopoly,
chance, and the reading railroad,
catch a ride on the rhombus!

As an escape vehicle,
I can assure you it's quite robust.
Escapism for the escapist
is bliss,
the part that's the art
of the escape artist.
It's the alchemy that makes up me,
a thief among us,
taking great pains
to catch a ride on the great freight train,
that robust bus
known as the rhombus.

Part IV
Purgatory for the Pontificatory

> "As we know,
> there are known knowns.
> There are things we know we know.
> We also know
> there are known unknowns.
> That is to say,
> we know there are some things
> we do not know.
> But there are also unknown unknowns,
> the ones we don't know
> we don't know."
>
> -Donald Rumsfeld

Purgatory for the Pontificatory

One should not confuse
the belief that's believable to believe
with, within reason,
what's reasonable to conclude,
something often misconstrued.

As life forms are really just highly complicated
versions of computer programs, of which we are only now even beginning
to understand and produce the most basic types,
We still have not yet reached a level of sophistication
and technology to create and translate these machines
into conscious or even unconscious organic beings.
For many, the very thought in unconscionable!
However, given the astonishing level of advancement
in the field of robotics in just the last 50 years,
it ought not seem out of the realm of possibilities
that it will be possible to achieve in the next
several thousand years, an insignificant period,
in the 'brief history of time'.
It is out of this where the idea stems
that those out there millions of years more advanced,
could have genetically engineered the seeds
which evolved into us. To which, the natural, logical response would be:
"So what?!" Simply saying that something "could have" happened
doesn't elevate it to a level of proper scientific theory
which should be taught to impressionable young minds
on equal footing with the best explanations we have at the current time,
explanations which at least have old fashioned concrete
evidence supporting them.
And to that I'd have to say that I agree,
but I still think it's worth exploring. Though, I wouldn't go as
far as to claim I'm officially an advocate of intelligent design,
(I didn't just fall off the turnip truck).
And I'm not at all religious, and as such the portrait
of so-called almighty creators as a couple of
B- science experimenters(a generous grade for all of humanity's flaws)
is something I don't find the least bit insulting.
I don't have a dog in that hunt.

Still, prior to the posterity
there is probably always an abundance of the preposterous.
Setting aside the orwellianly worded geometry
and the gimmickry of irreducible complexity,
yes, it's true that "intelligent design"
began mainly as a re-branding of creationism
to make it more marketable to a new generation
of makes and models, but that doesn't mean that
coincidentally the scientifically curious mind
might think they've stumbled onto something
(and not just a sociological study of those
born from rustic communities).
I can't say that I have any bone to pick
with evolution in particular, other than the curious nature
of man's curiosity towards the origin of his existence,
a trait that of all species, only humans appear to possess.
Not quite an atheist, but more a mysterian,
I prefer to think
it's like that episode of the twilight zone
with the dolls in the bin, orphaned,
looking to discover who or what they are
and how they've come to exist.
We're the five characters in search of an exit.
the unloved,
humans.

But alas,
one should not confuse
the belief that's believable to believe
with, within reason,
what's reasonable to conclude,
something often misconstrued.

Monkey Steals The Peach

See the
monkey see-monkey do,
how he mimics your every move.
See the
monkey see-monkey do
Watch him steal the peach from you

I've always liked The Monkees
better than The Beatles.
This is not to say that I think
The Monkees are "better" than
The Beatles.
I just like them better.
The Monkees are better than the Beatles much in the same way that
"Battlestar Galactica" was a cheap rip off of "Star Wars",
but ironically is actually so much better than "Star Wars"
(for a variety of reasons which I will decline to explain),

The Monkees were a manufactured illusion,
but their music, which to a great extent
wasn't even their music, stood the test of time
thus validating their existence.
Which means there was something there
between those four guys who didn't really
know each other.
The Monkees talent was their ambiance, the one thing
about them that mostly really came from them,
that makes me love the experience of listening to them.
I've always preferred illusion to reality,
not naively or merely out of ignorance, a refusal to believe,
rather I just simply would have preferred that the illusion,
in it's superiority, was actually the reality,
while still grounded by the fact that it isn't and most likely never will be.
The Beatles always seemed too perfect, too smug, too preachy, too
 depressing, too left wing, their music towards the end
too much a loss of innocence, which relates too intricately to the
 realities(as they view them) of the real world, and thus ruins the
 escapist's experience. I 'm not fond of real life and the real world in
 general (both the place and the show).

And so… I've never really liked the Beatles.
It's just way too easy to be able to,
whereas The Monkees are mediocre, easily unlikable,
not taken seriously by anyone and
therefore something I can relate to.

With the Beatles, it's like David Bowie;
One time I was in a car and the girl driving was going to put in a cd,
and she asked, "Do you guys like David Bowie?"
The other guy in the car responded with the obvious;
 "Who doesn't like David Bowie?"
As if to say "Of course. Everyone loves Bowie , right?."
(I do happen to like David Bowie)
Everyone loves The Beatles, right?

When you prefer The Monkees you're
rooting for the underdog, for mediocrity's
endless quest for respect.
And their songs are great, just like them.
The Monkees were able to master the art of masterpiece illusion,
and make some pretty damn cool music in the process
almost as a side effect.
From that illusion, they created something real,
for the disillusioned contrarian,
their enduring appeal.

Mind Probe

Mind you, perhaps you should
mind your p's and q's,
for the things you are thinking,
imagining me doing,
much less thinking,
bizarre things, uniquely disturbing
keep in mind,
this is all happening in your mind,
and not mine!

The Situation Room

The situation is this.
The situationalists believe a person
is a product of, and his behavior is influenced by,
his situation.
I am not a situationalist.
I am a situationalist criticalist!
Since the situations that influence,
are quite often self created.
If a precarious person,
gets himself into a precarious situation
which then influences him to behave precariously,
like the chicken and the egg,
was then his original situation the origin that made him precarious
to begin with, originally?
If this is true, as the situationalist would argue,
then everything has already been predetermined,
thus making any attempt at self determination
in making decisions,
a pointless exercise in futility.
The situationalist belief, is really
just a way to absolve people in the 21st century of all responsibility
for their actions and their opposite reactions,
polarity both positively and negatively,
both the blame and the credit for the do's and don'ts
of all they achieve.
It's as though everything has already been mapped out,
and people have little to know control over themselves.

To a significant degree, people are
most certainly influenced by their situation.
But willing and able,
the stubborn and strong willed will overcome them from within,
armed with the skill of self discipline.
This, done in strict non compliance and complete defiance
of the self defeating defeatist situationalist,
who is left with nothing to say but "touché!"

For let it be known, I earned my personality!

Generalize

Generally speaking,
sweeping generalizations are something to be brushed aside as ignorance.
But as an aside,
the truths they can reveal should
equally not be ignorantly swept under the rug.
Stereotypes exist for a reason,
for many, some good, some not so much.
And while exceptions are likely,
just as the belief in a utility in generalizations
is itself an exception to the conventional wisdom…
One who values time
must have some sort of screening process
if he is to be a productive individual.
The same applies to societies.
Since there will almost always be exceptions,
the question is not whether or not everyone in a certain group fits
the negative stereotype it has been given,
but rather,
whether the amount of people who don't fit the stereotype are enough
to justify tolerating the ones who do.

A Plethora

I think people should be forced
to take intelligence tests to determine
whether they are suitable for breeding.
That may sound harsh or unreasonable,
but I'm not talking about rigorous,
Rhodes scholarly examinations here.
I'm sure a simple fifth grade level aptitude test
would do just fine as
I see a plethora of people out there
reproducing who appear unable to
solve the most basic
multiplication problems.

Conspiratorial Theorem

I have a "theory" on the theorists
who promote and genuinely believe in conspiracy theories.
Firstly, they lack the skills
of critical thinking and deductive reasoning,
but more importantly,
it's more important to mention that
their lives are remarkably uninteresting and unimportant,
as this lays the groundwork for everything.
They compensate by rationalizing,
finding comfort in the notion that
amazed amidst the maze of their boring lives
they have finally stumbled onto something.
They see themselves as being privy
to some vital secret that's been uncovered,
that only they and a few others are aware of,
and that this somehow provides evidence of their own lives' significance.
I can offer no tangible evidence for this theory as
it's just based on eyewitness accounts, and unnamed sources
which technically means it wouldn't even qualify as a theory,
scientifically. Neither would most conspiracy theories.
But I do believe it, logically.
but religiously? Not really.
Rather, it's just some good old fashioned inductive reasoning

Progress

With nature, cooperating.
like the martians discovered,
the secret of being happy
is just to be-
for me I contend
that's not quite enough.
happiness, bliss,
with those contents,
to be content
I'm discontent.
It is less a preference
than progress,
the fruition of things curious.

Wise Men and The Fool

There's an old saying that
a "wise man requires very little to be happy
while a fool's heart is never content".
Perhaps unbeknownst to such wise men,
some people are willing to bear being miserable
in order to achieve progress.
That's how the west was won!
Subsequent prevalence of apologists
and revisionists,
and the absence of that pioneering spirit
in the year 2001,
is why mankind is going nowhere,
stalling but for a stalwart few.

It leaves one wondering,
which is the wise man,
and which is the fool?

And yet watching other people plod along
on their shallow quests, hellbent,
their greedy aspirations never quite met,
with each new purchase they can't afford…
they're satisfaction always lies in the next,
somewhere in the breath ahead.
After all you've been through, seeing yourself in their
endless loop, suddenly, the wise man with his marbles,
or in the forest playing the flute,
though he hasn't changed and barely moved
no longer looks quite the dupe.

And in a way he's just like me and you,
both the wise man and the fool.

Hypothesis of Hypotheticals

Sometimes we dwell upon
the hypotheticals
which don't have real consequences.
That's what makes them
not quite real.
What would you do, really?
But if one takes them
as an alternate reality
and in their view,
considers them seriously
a litmus test in which a true believer
truly believes,
then one must answer always
ever so carefully
for the consequences can be very

Boy Who Lied Wolf

A great way
to escape the predicament
of having to tell someone an unpleasant truth
is to tell a few small lies first.
You make them obvious
and let the person think they've caught you in the act
of perpetuating these minor fabrications.
Then when you turn to finally tell them
the awful truth, look them in the eye
and have your moment of sincerity.
You tell them the honest to god's truth only
honestly they won't believe you.
They won't even be upset because
they'll think it's just another bold faced lie.
It's like "the boy who cried wolf" in reverse.

Phoenix City

People always talk about making their cities "cool", but the
main reason Phoenix will never be "cool" in it's current form
is because people here always refer to the state name rather than the city.
If you think of great cities like Chicago,
people never say 'I'm moving to Illinois'.
Just think how lame that would sound.
Instead they say "I'm moving to Chicago".
People from Phoenix always just say they
live in Arizona, which sounds absolutely terrible.
So one should always promote the city
rather than the state. Note even the dreadful sports team names:
the Arizona Cardinals, the Arizona Diamondbacks.
Even in the once great state of California, people
cite their heritage with their respective cities(or regional locale at the
 very least): San Francisco, Los Angeles, San Diego, Orange County,
 Sacramento, "the valley", Laguna Beach etc.
The exception to this rule is of course New York,
because the city has the same name as the state.
Always when people ask me 'So How's Arizona?',
I reply with "Arizona? Oh I wouldn't know, I live in Phoenix".
So no one can ever say I never did anything for this place.

Phoenix Down

One thing I've always hated about Phoenix is this idea that it's cool to
be white trash. The white trash lifestyle is somehow romanticized here.
The tackiest dive bars are the so called "hip" establishments.
The most popular local celebrities are all the trashiest, sleaziest people
you can imagine(and accept this as a futility, complimentary).
People "glam"orize things like butt rock and boots,
(and I'm not talking about mod boots which actually ARE neato).
Generally the loudest, most lowbrow, totally hicked out anything is
what people in Phoenix take seriously. Even the local "publications"
don't hesitate to promote this attitude, drunk off the idea and desperately
salivating at the prospect that there might be something resembling a
scene developing. In the 90's when talking and acting like black
gangsters was the big thing, my friends and I used to joke that in the
year 2000's it would be cool to be white trash, and it actually came
true!

Unnatural Selection

The most intelligent argument for design,
without saying much,
is intelligence itself,
since intelligence does not appear to be evolutionary.
It doesn't make complete sense that out of
all these millions of species,
only one has achieved this
remarkably advantageous trait,
intelligence. Maybe it is simply man's decisive victory in
nature's version of "Monopoly."
If indeed intelligence is not evolutionary,
(a subject often immersed in controversy)
but rather,
if it's an acquired property,
then from where, what or whom
did we acquire it from?
and why were humans, of all creatures
great and small
unnaturally selected for it?

Design Process

Intelligent design and atheism
are not mutually exclusive
positions.
ID advocates believe with the evidence
of intelligence,
you can make an inference
to a designer rather than natural processes
to explain our existence.
It is entirely possible that we were
designed by some higher life form,
but as skeptics and critical thinkers
we simply prefer not to infer
anything,
would rather not interfere with the process
except to signal
that further research is needed.

Eye of the Perceived Valuer

Most likely, there's a huge difference in the quality of a five dollar pair
  of shoes and a hundred and seventy-five dollar pair of shoes,
but there's really not much difference between a hundred and seventy-
five dollar pair of shoes and a two-thousand dollar pair of shoes.
Unless one is made out of an extraordinarily rare material,
both probably cost about the same to manufacture.
When people buy a hyper expensive item, they're often doing so to
  appear sophisticated, chic, and as possessing a sort of "worldly taste for
  the finer things".Rather than worldly, as they appear to their peers,
sadly they just look foolish and gullible in the eyes of
anyone who understands anything about this sordid sort of marketing.

Rather than buying at a percentage above cost, they are buying on
perceived value, whereby some people basically got together and decided
they want to sell "two-thousand dollar" pairs of shoes to people who
want to buy "two-thousand dollar" pairs of shoes, and priced them
accordingly. So in our eyes, the people who fall for such marketing
tactics are spending money to illustrate that critical thinking and
reasoning were not the critical factors in their accruing of the wealth
which provided them the "luxury" of being able to purchase expensive
shoes. The common defense of said individuals is the eye opening "so
what if I like nice things?" thus further revealing their naivety, as they
equate "nice" with merely "more expensive," and inexpensive with low
quality, while discounting all other variables like production costs,
labor, country of origin, ingredients and raw materials used, sleaziness
of the company owner, etc.

Let me be clear and state that I'm not advocating that one should
  purchase cheap shoes,
as there's a fine line between inexpensive and tacky,
just as one exists between glamorous and gaudy.
I'm merely stating that people should think critically when buying,
as the difference between a modestly price pair of shoes
and a less modestly priced pair, is unlikely to be robust enough to justify
  the astronomical leap in price, but is likely to be a reflection of the
  modesty of the buyer. Beware!

But if the buyer believes, and their desired social results with the item are
  actually achieved, then who are we when we perceive they have been so
  easily deceived?

From One Small Corner

Living in America, or pretty much anywhere,
one inevitably encounters in their daily peregrinations,
some that are so unconscious of the amount
of physical space they take up in the world,
excessively exceeding in their own excess,
but oh so smug in their pontifications
of the excess of others, whom they would gladly get the better of.
Like the family of twelve with their children in line-1,2,…3,
they've had a few too many
centers of tootsie roll pops,
the wife, a licentious howler,
the average large rude man,
a blow pop with a blown top,
such is the bloviating blow up doll
a hot air balloon,
that far from being able to go around the world in eighty days,
when in the bathroom, often cannot even see it's own shoes.
metaphorically and figuratively
a blob of a human being
of epic, ectoplasmic proportions
and they are everywhere,
as far and wide as every uncharted grocery aisle.
There is plenty to be had,
but whatever sympathy for such creatures
is often squandered when they begin to feast their eyes
on what's near and dear to, even you.

Sinus of the Times

And so,
right now there's a battle going on against mucous!
And in this battle you are either with us
or you are with the mucous.
It's going to be a long war.
It's like the war on terrorism
We don't know when it will ever end.
We're told it may not even be over in our lifetime.
As citizens, we all need to be vigilant.
It's all we can do.

Part V
A Castler, Castling

"…and do forgive the ill manners of an old recluse."
–Walter Pidgeon,
Dr. Morbius in "The Forbidden Planet"

A Castler, Castling

Oh and how,
to be left alone.
a castler, castling,
minding his own.
A brick and mortar layer,
walling himself in
from within his lair,
a deep sea diver
with no desire to come up for
a breath of fresh air.

A castler, castling
at home alone
doing his own thing.
Of one small corner,
he's still the king.

Oh and how
To be left alone.
a castler, castling
minding his own.

A castler, castling,
who'll be in the castle
if you need anything.

Artificial Incrimination

Some people have a few skeletons in their closet.
Some people have more skeletons in their closet than others,
and will guard dearly,
their skeleton key.

It's always a delicate situation
when a friend's going through your things
and happens to stumble upon something incriminating.

If they mention that which they have found
which incriminates you,
then they have incriminated themselves
in the process,
for violating your privacy,
breaching your confidentiality,
and sacrificing their place amongst those deemed trustworthy.

If on the other hand,
they refrain from saying anything,
a cloud will hang over,
as by not mentioning it
they must act as if nothing's out of the ordinary,
forever behaving partially artificially,
cursed with the burden of self secrecy.

Such an unpleasant circumstance leaves one wondering,
is satisfying one's curiosity worth sacrificing one's place
among the trustworthy,
or forever bearing the burden of self secrecy?
Perhaps those who are doing the finding,
will find out for themselves,
what it's like to have to hide something incriminating.

Some people have a few skeletons in their closet.
Some people have more skeletons in their closet than others,
and will guard dearly,
their skeleton key.

Chess Mate

I'm playing a game of chess
against myself
I can't win,
I can't lose,
I've forgotten whose move
it was.
What's mine is ours
minus what's yours
I put myself in check
mate,
it's how I make
myself
an improvement.

The Open Minded

There's an old saying;
"It's important to be open minded,
but don't be so open minded that your brains fall out…"

People often tell me
I need to be more open minded,
but they themselves perhaps aren't
as open minded as they'd like to think.
otherwise they would be more
open to the idea of being closed minded.

Hider in the House

Be mindful of those in their mission to keep things hidden.
Before thinking about someone,
who is thought to be hiding something,
and how they can't get away with hiding anything from you...

Before thinking that someone can't hide anything,
keep in mind
you may not have found all of the hiding things.

Kept

Some secrets are better left kept
some boxes just left,
unchecked.
some people to their own devices
to indulge themselves
self indulgent with their own vices.
Some would rather keep still
being kept to themselves.
Still some things have been left
some things different
something's different, same difference,
but some things have been left
that should have been kept.

Annoying Midi

What others would figure,
what they would, but wouldn't really
consider,
what they would figure is just an annoying midi,
I might think is a pretty enchanting melody.
What they would say is thoroughly annoying
is something I could enjoy thoroughly.
Perhaps they'd think I'm just amused easily,
that I could enjoy the tune of an annoying midi.
But if the ambiance is appealing to a side
inside of me,
an innocence,
and if the melody is in an invoked memory,
then maybe one could see the beauty
others miss,
what they dismiss
as just an annoying midi.

Fight or Space Flight

The culmination
of the accumulation of instances
whereby invasion of personal space
was the culprit
and those not conscious
of the concept of it,
instead unconsciously
thinking of only themselves
while not self-conscious!

This blatant,
(to like minded purported self-enlightened),
obviously oblivious
disregard and disrespect for time and space
by the vast majority
and overwhelming minorities!
is reciprocated only
by the lonely dreamer's narcissism
his cavalier indifference
to human life.
seeing already an abundance of it
gobs and gobs
in the form of blobs
everywhere,
blobs dot com.

and a hopelessness for progress
without first doing something drastic.
seeking an escape,
but feeling beyond it.
While others waste time with war,
he looks for space,
toward it,
to conquer or be conquered by it.

Whichever Way You're Not

It appears you're coming, and going my way.
Therefore I'll go another way.
Can't look the other way,
The thought of you being near,
just the thought,
makes me feel not so hot.
Get set, ready or no,
I'll just go whichever way you're not.

Knowing where you are,
helps me decide where not to be,
makes it easier,
easier for me.
Like someone walking at the same speed,
I'll slow my pace,
make the opposing move,
whatever I have to
to be opposite from you so,
get set, ready or no,
I'll just go whichever way you're not.

This world's not big enough for all of us.
Someone save the select few,
make something beautiful,
start anew.
But what right do I have to get rid of you?
I've got the will,
without a way to make it so.
I'll just go whichever way you're not.

The Way In

That's a horrible place to stand
right there
right where you are
you're right where I need to be
what a horrible place to stand
for me

Unsolicited Talkers

On the show Seinfeld, they used to talk about "close talkers",
people who get uncomfortably close when they talk to you
thus invading your personal space. Those are pretty annoying,
but my issue has always been with "unsolicited talkers",
strangers who come up and try to talk to you even when
you've not made eye contact, given the slightest indication you wish to
  speak to them, or even acknowledged their presence, and
have in fact even gone out of your way to avoid them
at the first sign of them approaching. Yet still they will ask you for
  money, or shout some rude, vulgar or inappropriate comment, totally
oblivious and inconsiderate of the fact that you switched to the opposite
  sidewalk for a reason. I think a lot of people need to be put in cages.
Like when you're walking down the street minding your own business,
whimsically daydreaming, and someone yells something obnoxious at
  you from a car window, that person should be put in a cage and fed
  slabs of meat. People always say "oh just ignore them",
but you can't ignore them! That's the whole problem.
And why should it be my responsibility
to have to deal with it at all?
If all those types of uncivilized humans were sent away,
then the rest of us could just lie around and play
and eat pomegranate in hammocks.

Guilt in Slow Motion

The people you meet can turn out to be quite neat,
if you take the time to know them.
Everyone has their own galaxy going on inside their heads.
Some galaxies are more vast and contain more stars than others,
but if you take the time to explore, you could discover
something interesting in someone you did not think would be.
From afar, it's hard to see,
individually, human beings.
For as a group we appear clearly, unworthy.

If you take the time to get to know them, objectively,
the people you meet can turn out to be quite neat,
leaving you and I feeling guilty,
ashamed of our previous feelings.

Abort Time

I don't really have a problem with abortion.
My only real problem with it is that there
are too few of them, and that the
type of people who should be having them aren't
(mainly the degenerates of society),
while intelligent and otherwise fully capable individuals
whom could produce civil and productive members of society,
upstanding citizens and so on, are much more likely to have
abortions(or at the very least choose not to reproduce).

Some argue that abortion leaves the sanctity
of human life in ruins, while to others the absence of abortion
is ruining the sanctity of life for so many already living humans!
-and drowning out the voice of the
few who realize there are too many people
here already.

The New Pioneers

The new pioneers will be the escape artists,
those who rebel and flee from
the tyranny of the majority of walmartists and breeding heartists.
See, the world remains a lost cause,
so why should they remain there?
Instead they'll set sail for a new place,
a rock, an island or an islet,
somewhere where there's peace and quiet,
and call it their temporary home.
with a metaphoric force field, they'll
shield themselves, build a new society,
and plead to be with diplomatic niceties,
left alone..
Research and build a sophisticated base,
and blast themselves off into space
in search of a new way for humans to start again
settle in a new place,
like settlers often do,
and even while they will make
they'll try to learn from our past mistakes.

Southern Strategy

There was a civil war game for the original Nintendo called "North And South." It was one of the first real time strategy games ever made. One had the option to control either the Union Army or the Confederates. I would almost always play as the South, doing my small part in an effort to try and change history. Part of this decision was likely due to my undeniable contrarian nature, and a natural tendency to side with the underdog. In other words, had the South won the war I would probably be playing as the North.

Having stated that, I've often felt that the country would have been better served if the south would have won the war. The question of the freedom of state and local governments to form the types of societies their people want to live in, is one that has never been resolved. It just so happens that the civil war had to fought over the most abhorrent example of this, slavery. Had it been any other issue such as taxes, trade, religion, anything other than the indefensible practice of slavery, the South could have been able to claim the moral high ground for simply wanting to have their own government and laws, their own cultural identity.

Had the South won the war, slavery would likely have been abolished anyway just as it had been nearly everywhere throughout the world as nations evolved into more civilized societies. And it's important to note that the North was not fighting to end slavery but to preserve the union. They only started to introduce and emphasize the moral issue of slavery midway through the war when it became clear it would make their cause appear more just.

That being said, I'm not so sure I have any great romantic affinity for the South personally. My own experience with southern culture is for the most part limited to having once had biscuits and gravy at the Atlanta airport while waiting for a connecting flight.

But imagine if the south had indeed won, people would have had a choice of which America to live in. Freedom is not merely individual freedom to do what one wants but also the freedom to live in the type of society one wants to live in. If some Christians want to have a paradise city full of religious wackos and impose their rules and values on those who live there, that's fine, just the same as it would be if the antithesis of gays, libertarians or socialists created a society which theirs is the accepted ethos. This gives a person options as to how he wants to live and leaves him free of being forced to deal with things he does not wish to have to encounter in everyday life. If there are different places with different rules, it prevents a universal or total society of which there is no escape and prevents a "last man" type of situation in the world. In politics as in love or life, intentions can often have the opposite effect. In other words, libertarianism without borders can lead to a lack of freedom, lack of diverse societies, a lack of choice.

And that's the other reason for playing as the south in the classic NES game, "North and South," and probably no less futile than any more practical attempt to prevent the country (or even the world) from progressing into a homogenized society of diversity, where oxymoronically all societies within are free from diversity of thought, and of different ways of life.

Force Field

They don't see,
but know it's there.
They'll discover their strong will
won't penetrate,
can't break the seal,
what they can but can't feel
the force field,
a shield that protects my true self
from becoming someone else

The Veldt

My self,
along with the size, make
and shape of it's shell,
often shelled,
is partly the result
of the sum
of all the pelts I've taken
while wandering
on the veldt

Screwed, Blued, and Tattooed

Never have I been fond of tattoos,
or for that matter, tattooed dudes,
and if you have one, it's a
pre-judgment against you.
I think they're trashy,
and if that's not bad enough,
they ruin your versatility.
Once you have one, you might as well have two
cause you can never be anything else
but a tattooed dude.
I must admit,
I have liked a few tattooed girls before,
very few,
but it was in spite of the fact
they had tattoos,
and not because of it.
Besides, they mostly only like "guys with tattoos".

I do have some tattooed friends.
Some of my best friends have tattoos.
So you can't say I'm racist against tattoos.

Life on Mars

One of the only redeeming qualities
of the city of Phoenix is that living there,
you can sometimes just pretend you're on Mars.
A city in the desert,
the natural landscape and general aesthetic
are very similar in appearance to the red planet.
The dust storms,
the mad-made nature
of the futuristic architecture
and of course the canals!
Basically Phoenix resembles what I
would envision Mars to look like
if it had more of an atmosphere-

but not much more of an atmosphere.

Democracy, Demography, Demagoguery, Demigoddery

Democracy is being undone by demography.
The main problem with democracy is that everyone gets a vote.
Stupid people are reproducing at a much higher rate than intelligent
people, because smart people grasp what an awesome responsibility
having children is, and limit themselves to procreating only what they
can contain within their modest means, whatever it may be. Therefore,
one can induce that impoverished, uneducated people at some point will
make up the majority, in which case they will ironically make the case
that government programs (funded by taxing responsible or non
breeders) are needed to provide for their children, not because children
are unaffordable, but because they had more than they could afford, and
so they demand others pick up the slack and fund their experiments in
sexual activity.

And who are we to say? As they will be in the majority, the heathens
will make a mad grab for whatever they can get their hands on! That is,
until the dwindling remaining who are supporting these folks no longer
make up enough of a demographic atm machine to cover for the
growing epidemic of babyfever, which will lead to bankrupt
institutions, and even more uneducated masses, tomfoolery, and
madeupwordery than future tribes of the world can shake a stick at!

One could always argue that those people don't vote, but actually they
do vote, just not in the same proportions. And there are in fact endless
ad campaigns and promotions, which actually encourage uninformed
pointy heads to vote as a form of civic duty, when in fact they should be
encouraged not to. At some point there will be so damn many of them
that even that small percentage that participates in the election process
will be enough to overtake the rest of us.

Intelligent people of the future will simply figure out a way to wall
themselves in somewhere, and create their own mini-empires where they
will try to maintain a semblance of an existence amidst the tattered
shreds of civilization. Heading out only for a few supplies, they will
seek the delicate balance between the suffocation of loneliness and the
threat posed from mindless zombies, that of being metaphorically eaten
alive.

Cheese and Crackers

In due time paying my dues,
time spent alone,
in time I've learned to live with myself,
perhaps just in the nick of time.

For me, the fruition of self contentment is
a monumental achievement,
of continental proportions.
Always able to entertain myself,
for years I could not contain,
indeed could not restrain myself
in deeds involving love,
obsessed with the obsession of it,
I willingly signed over the deed to my heart and soul.
Not believing in myself, but rather the belief
that being by myself, was not so great.

But by a stroke of luck, or more likely,
my own tendency toward idiosyncrasy,
I tend to end up that way anyway.
Through many years I suffered and ached as a result of heartbreak,
but an amazing thing happened by coincidence of my loneliness.
That is, in time I've learned to live with myself.
It's what everyone needs to learn for themselves-.

Just cozy up with a nice book,
maybe some cheese and crackers

Out of His Shell

Just recently,
I've come to the realization
that I must have missed out entirely on
the whole "being a man" thing.
you know, just skipped right over it.
I think I went straight from boy to
"shell of a man."

Scumtown

Have a look at the havoc of this place.
Oh, I bet it used to be great,
but just look at it now.
It's a scumtown.

A long time ago, while watching the James Bond movie
"Goldfinger," in a studio apartment in
what was once West Hollywood,
during an opening sequence, when the camera closes in on
a spectacular resort in Miami
(always notice the beautiful dive),
I uttered this seemingly obvious remark,
"I bet Miami was a great place back then...before all the immigrants."
My friend whom I was with seemed mildly irritated
by the comment for what he perceived as it's implied
"subtle racism." And maybe he was right,
but it's something one could go on to say
about a great many once great places.
On my first full day in Los Angeles,
my first impression was a Sears on Santa Monica and Western
which I would come to refer to as "third world Sears."
There were hordes of people stampeding throughout the place,
and clothing strewn about everywhere, with reckless disregard
for the generally accepted and often excessively anal standards
of your average department store. This is not your average
department store, but as the US continues its transition toward
becoming a third world country,
where such refugee camp swap meets represent normalcy,
it soon may be. I wasn't thinking about that, though. All I could think of
was that at one time it must have been a wonderful store,
and anyone involved in the building of the building
or who had worked there in it's heyday
would be appalled and saddened
at the looted corpse of an establishment it had become.
More comically, there is a place on Sunset called "The All American
Burger,"
where there literally did not appear to be one American working there.
But of course appearance isn't everything, so there may have been.

The Los Angeles experience is one that can be summed up
in the episode of "The Simpsons" where they go to Hollywood,
and as the tour bus passes a famous landmark, the tour guide
points toward a seedy vacant lot with a few bums milling about
and says; "Uh, for those of you who always wanted to see the famous
 Brown Derby restaurant...that's where it used to be."
When I was a kid we lived on a street with
a string of townhouses, where everyone knew each other, and
all the kids(and often parents) played together in each other's yards.
Everybody on the block was like your family, and every house was like
your house with the only difference being that yours was the one you
slept in at night.

There's no question that there are thousands of neighborhoods as yet
unaffected, where all that stuff still happens, new places being
constructed where in the future it will happen, and of course it probably
already didn't happen back then in places where it had once happened.
Still, it's always sad to see something doesn't happen and will never
again happen somewhere that it used to happen.
What's happening?

It's like in "Back to the Future II" when
Marty Mcfly travels to 2015, and is elated to discover
he will live "Hilldale,"(a lush neighborhood in his own time)
until he learns it is really just a future ghetto,
just as in the first film when he goes to 1955 and sees
how "Lyon Estates" was a promising new development in the 50's,
but would become a subpar subdivision by the 1980's.
That's about enough lenses to desensitize more than one of one's senses.
After all, it's tense enough even without all the tenses.

These days it seems one can't walk 50 feet without being harassed by an
aggressive bum asking for money, or some self entitled hurricane Katrina
refugee who responds with threats and belligerence no matter whether
his request is politely declined or even accepted.
For those with number counter syndrome, they can never have enough.
They always want more numbers to count.
To them, the ambiance doesn't.
But to some of us, ambiance matters!
and there's no arguing with the feeling of an experience.
It is what it is.

Spending an afternoon watching Cary Grant
mountaineering about Mount Rushmore in "North By Northwest",
and directly following that by a trip to one's nearest
gihugic mega mall (and I say "nearest" because these behemoths are not
worthy of the term "local"), one can intuitively, inductively, reasonably
observe, this place has gone down the tubes. And if not,
then they don't know or don't care what they won't miss.

To that people always say something along the lines of
"the 50's and 60's weren't really like the way they were portrayed in
movies." And yes, it's true that life for all wasn't exactly as depicted
in old Rock Hudson and Doris Day films,
(after all Rock Hudson was gay!)
But so what?!
It may not have been entirely like that, but whatever it was,
was certainly nothing like this.
Either wall it off, or wall me in.
There's nothing out there.
Nothing left but to be left
to the sanctuary of one's own imagination within.

Have a look at the havoc of this place.
Oh, I bet it used to be great,
but just look at it now.
It's a scumtown

The Boy and the Painting of a Treehouse

This is the true story of a boy
that dreamed up a boy(his imaginary self)
who often stared at
the painting of a treehouse,
a painting of a treehouse, that if only he could have(the treehouse),
he would never come out.
And all of the people would shout
"Wherever you are,
come out! come out!"
There's nothing out there, he thought.
He would rather stay in and dream of the boy
(his imaginary self) who often stared
at the painting of a treehouse.
All of his friends and family thought
it was bizarre and antisocial behavior. They would
have preferred he moved on to more practical pursuits.
Suffice to say they didn't approve
of the boy's dream of the boy(his imaginary self)
who often stared at the painting of a treehouse,
though it's harmless enough, they thought.
Probably just a phase.
But still it continues on to this day.
At a certain point in the dream,
one day the boy mysteriously disappears,
and no one seems to know where he is.
Assuming he's somewhere hiding out,
his friends and loved ones begin to shout,
"Wherever you are,
come out! come out!"
They scour the world, unable to find him,
Largely though, no one would notice.
Until finally a young girl looked up and discovered for herself
a painting of a girl dreaming of a girl(her imaginary self)
who often stared at a painting of the
boy in a treehouse.

Part VI
Bionic at Best

"I told myself I wanted to make an artificial man,
but I think what I really wanted was to build another me,
only without all the drawbacks, a sort of reverse Jekyll and Hyde"
-George Gizzard as Walter Ryder
The Twilight Zone, episode 103 "In His Image"

Bionic

A partition in the fruition it would seem
possibly, a partial redemption
for past failures and shattered dreams
alas!
one finally achieves!
in his aspiration to become at last
an imperfect machine,
impervious to the ridiculous notion(but not completely)
of uncontrolled emotions.
A representation of a psychological overcoming
of the temptation biological.
Come one, come all!
Step right up! Step right up!
Witness the final transformation,
the creature now bestowed with an eye for focus, robust
as he becomes in essence a bionic man,
equipped with, one might have guessed,
a bionic implant, an uncanny ability to plant himself,
firmly grounded.
In reality, the new reality,
he is a product of self direct input in a system otherwise gone kaput.
A microchip, in place of what was once the shoulder chip,
has become the primary storage facility for fond memories,
with the conscience, conscious, coldly calculating it's calculations.
A quest success,
at best bionic, bionic at best.
with the shoulder to cry on, now the cold of cryonic
For some, it's a bitter pill to swallow.
Others curious, and eager to discover
what's behind that cryogenic exterior,
step in line looking to assume
their rightful place amidst the missed,
in an attempt to circumvent the circuitry or
pull him out of character with
the tractor beam of distraction.
But rest assured, with a little luck,
while that truth does not compute,
the decoding of the decoder ring may
convey the message,
this one will not self-destruct.

Rydia

"I think I have fallen in love with a video game character!"
One shouldn't believe it's so absurd
that in the future
people could fall in love with
video game characters,
machines, robots and the like,
or look for ways to transfer their consciousness
into virtual realities as they become more attractive
environments than the current dimension.

As time goes on, people are seemingly becoming less human,
less romantic, less surreal and ever more material,
career oriented, less interested,
while robots become even more complicated,
with their creators coming closer
to creating a creation that
more closely mimics
the human complex.

While humans continue trending mindless, careless,
computers are slowly mutating into computants,
behaving more like the better of
what's inside of us.

As such, it's not unfathomable that the line
could begin to blur,
and that for a romantic guy/girl,
a love affair with a machine
might be more fulfilling, than with
a cold, vapid, empty humanoid.

"I promise,
I'm not a dysfunctional person,
I'm fully functional."

Illusion as Reality

Dreaming of another-
reality,
illusion manifests itself
attempting to elude
reality.
and in doing so
quite possibly
can become
reality-
if the illusion is convincing enough to be perceived as
reality.
for as perception changes actuality
ironically, gradually
eventually,
suddenly!
illusion is now the
reality

A Day at the Zoo

"Never though that I'd be acting humanoid
that ain't the simian thing to do
humanoids go frantic but before things get romantic
and I'm going humanoid over you!

If I thought that you'd enjoy it
I'd stop trying to avoid it
I'm going humanoid over you!" – Return to the Planet of the Apes

Inspiration for humanity can originate from the most unlikely of sources,
such as in the case of "Return To the Planet of the Apes"
(created by none other than the creators of the Pink Panther!),
the short lived 1975 cartoon series based on the popular Planet of the
Apes film franchise, which had been based on the novel by Pierre Boulle.

The intense and colorful opening sequence, a montage
of stills and it's accompanying theme stand as a strangely moving
yet completely forgotten and never appreciated work of 70's pop art.

The premise of RTTPOTA is familiar territory.
This time, three astronauts: Bill Hudson, Jeff Allen,
and Judy Franklin get trapped in the future where mankind
has destroyed itself, and the apes have taken over.
The astronauts spend the majority of the episodes
trying to protect the remaining primitive humans,
and lead them out of the caves and on a long treacherous journey to
"New Valley," a supposed place of safety where they can
"build pueblos the way the Indians did in New Mexico and Arizona."
All the while, they must stay ahead of, outsmart and sometimes fend off
attacks from the apes and their cunning and determined, "General Urko".
Oh and that General Urko, what a character! He is portrayed as
something of a belligerent, bumbling fool, but in reality he is incredibly
intuitive and nearly always correct in his suspicions of what his enemies
are up to.

Occasionally the humans must venture into Ape City to seek the help
of ape scientists and "simiantarians" Cornelius and Zira, the only apes
not openly hostile toward the humanoids.

Dr. Zaius emerges once again as a somewhat ambiguous character
who always appears to know more than he lets on.
A calm and just(for an ape) leader and member of the Senate,
he represents a sort of "neutral" character,
somewhere in between the bellicose General Urko and the mild
Simiantarians, Zira and Cornelius.
His personal feelings are never made totally clear.
In stark contrast to the films, the underdwellers(a technologically
advanced society of hooded mutant humans who survived the war and
live underground) led by Krador, are a more peaceful breed whose only
wish is to live in harmony and one day return to "the green world above."
The underdwellers are infatuated with Judy
and refer to her only as "Usa"(pronounced 'oosa')
for they have a statue of her, an artifact of the 21st century engraved with
"Lost, USA" presumably erected after the astronauts' original
disappearance in space. The underdwellers hold the belief that "Usa" will
someday lead them out of the darkness and back to the surface.

"Return to the Planet of the Apes" it would seem does more for race
relations than anything the likes of "diversity training" ever could.
The cartoon series, like the films, humanizes and personifies all living
creatures (with the rare exception of prehistoric birds and giant sea
monsters). By portraying humans as having become a lower order of
species,(subservient to the now more sophisticated, apes) it serves as a
mirror image for humans as to how we've treated those once viewed as
different amongst are own kind. Whether it be the blacks, the indians, or
whomever, as best as a cartoon can, it places you in their shoes so you
may feel as they once did and often still do.

More importantly though, it's amazing how quickly humans can set aside
their petty cosmetic differences when faced with a threat posed by
another species, in this case the apes. Bill,(a white male) Judy,(a woman)
and Jeff,(a black man) represent three factions which have constantly
been squabbling with one another for centuries, and would likely be
bickering endlessly if they had nothing better to do.
Yet, they get along just fine here. Why?
Because they only see themselves as humans!
They don't subcategorize themselves, but instead leave behind the
subcategories themselves in the 20th century where they belong.
And I mean, if only Jeff Allen were running for president!...soft spoken,
contemplative, charismatic, decent, he's the antithesis of most of the
African American leaders and public figures of today.

Whatever happened to those modest, 70's sideburn sporting,
turtleneck wearing, medallion rocking, poetry reading, black American
men who spoke the king's English and everything. Oh how I want them
back. Sadly, many were apparently subsequently replaced
by all the gangsters, hip hoppers, and belligerent 'hoot and hollerers'.
Though something along these lines this could probably be said to relate
to all humanity. I just wish there were more men out there like Bill
Hudson and Jeff Allen.
Let me be the first to nominate Austin Stoker for president!
I would even risk the possibility of getting jury duty to vote for him.

While the creators of "The Pink Panther" won an Oscar for "The Pink
Phink" in 1964, "Return to the Planet of the Apes" was cancelled after a
mere 13 episodes. It barely registers as even a blip on the historical map
of American pop culture, and is critically remembered negatively,
if at all.

But as you can see, I often wonder about Bill, Jeff and Judy, and if and
where their personalities can be found in our world today.
As for the series itself, some of us see it not just as some non-essential
part of a dragged out money making franchise, a third rate afterthought,
but rather we see "Return to the Planet of the Apes" as a vastly
underappreciated gem,

...worthy of an academape award.

Alas

At last, the future is futuristic,
it's every bit as horrific,
magically magnificent
and twice as lonely as one used to anticipate,
the gadgetries, positively the politic,
all of it
finally fulfilling 1970's
science fiction prophecies,
but not for the specific,
still it's biologically mythic
terrifically centaurrific!
I love it, but hate this
world.
The future is now what was-
I wouldn't have missed it for the
mystic mystery,
to see what misery I had in store
and have to look forward to.

Flavorful

I'm not all that concerned with the flavor of food.
I wish I could just eat bricks of food,
they would come out of a machine
and would have everything you need,
shades of soylent green,
food like the kind astronauts eat
on a stick or in a small tube.
I used to just eat bricks of tofu,
and I would put cheese on it and vegenaise,
then place it in the microwave.
I could eat that every single day,
and it makes me feel like I'm in the future.

Wind-up Boy

If you can appreciate a good painting,
if you don't mind
falling in love with a painting
a beautiful image
but a painting nonetheless
with nothing behind it

It's all an illusion really
I'm like a house of cards,
carefully constructed and elaborate
like a labyrinth.
but a house of cards nonetheless
ever so fragile

If you can fall in love
with a painting of a person
more than just a caricature to be sure
a painting, where the eyes follow you
as you move across the room
you might just wind up
in a sanitarium
with the wind-up boy
wound and bound to you.

Characteristic

Someone told me it's not really like me.
that it was totally out of character,
but it isn't uncharacteristic of
me to say something out of character
when I'm in character.
It's part of my character,
being a man of character and all,
to do and say things
that might appear out of character.
I'm a real character like that.

Sun Makes Me Sneeze

Who needs natural light
just to see the world artificially?
My world's technicolor
just the way that I like my movies.

Sun makes me sneeze as it rises in the east,
don't care to look as far as the eye can see.
All things dark still appear bright to me

Let them stay outside and play
I've got it made in the shade.
While I won't let you in,
we can still be false friends.
Just please don't bother me.

Sun makes me sneeze as it rises in the east,
don't care to look as far as the eye can see.
All things dark still appear bright to me

Who needs natural life
just so you can live artificially?
see if you can picture this
sunless photosynthesis
in the land of technophobia.

Sun makes me sneeze as it rises in the east,
don't care to look as far as the eye can see.
All things dark still appear bright to me.

Wallflower

Inanimate, it's unanimous!
Let's hear it, objections not withstanding,
put your hands together for inanimate objects,
for it's unanimous(among some),
that intimately one functions inanimately,
which could mean any number of things.
I've been called a bench before
in a storm of resentment
for the contentment of being content
with just lounging around,
unwilling to venture far from the fort
of my comfort zone, to the forbidden
which in myself remains, but hidden.
But contrary to what some have aimed
to have claimed,
talking to me is a lot but not at all
like talking to a wall.
Without responding,
the mind in due process, does process everything
to the appropriate degree.
Whereas a wall is completely,
merely an inanimate object
that does absolutely nothing,
which even still, serves useful purposes.
So, I'm not exactly a wall after all
but rather an interactive wallflower,
just barely a grudgingly participating observer,
actively active only in protesting the act of activity
itself,
myself in a corner,
a broken tape recorder that records words,
rewinds and remembers,
but cannot fast forward.
Yes, I've been called a bench before,
with some truth conceded in the clamor
to the claimer of the claim.
a bench with maybe some semblance of a brain
but a bench the same.
Still, like I once remarked on a first date,
just don't expect to be entertained.

Curious

And I like the idea
that someday
after I'm long gone
and all but forgotten
if I am to be remembered at all,
you might for some reason see
"2001 A Space Odyssey"
and sit through it,
in it's entirety.
And perhaps you'll be curious
though not storm out…
like Rock Hudson, would say
"can someone please tell me
what all this is about?",
why it was always so interesting to me
that I could watch it on repeat for days,
and what it all means.
though I know you may not really care,
I'll know at least I never lost your curiosity and intrigue
and maybe you'll finally understand
and we'll have successfully communicated
in some third rate form of ESP,

and you'll remember me fondly
maybe, if I'm lucky,
with a hint of regret,
but really curiously,
it's curiosity
that's what's most important to me.

Mondo

Never mind.
Take me there!
If I had my way, this escapist
would be making his getaway
from the stress of the mad, mad world
to the grooviness of the mod, mod world.
Using only the crude time travel technology
of imagination and remote viewing
through vintage movies, old music,
mockumentaries and imaginary memories.

Nevertheless,
Take me there!
I'm embarking on a journey for posterity
to spend my remaining days
in a half witted wish
even if only for the ambiance
to live them out on the sunset strip in Los Angeles
in the summer of 1966.

The point being?
a recurring theme;
If the promise of the current "real" reality becomes empty enough,
then even the empty promise of a vividly imagined make-believe
can come to be more fulfilling, comparatively.

Sacrifice

As Kirk Douglas once said
while playing chess against Hector,
the robot in the film "Saturn 3",
"You can't teach them how to sacrifice."
It's easy to die for something,
or say you would.
Lots of guys would say they'd die for you,
some probably would.
But how many guys would say they'd kill for you?
Only one probably could.
To be willing to sacrifice someone else for your cause
is to be really cavalier about something though.

Terrorists blow themselves up everyday
for all sorts of worthless endeavors,
and yet their causes live on.
Yet when a few astronauts
accidentally perish while performing extraordinary scientific
feats in outer space,
many are willing to sacrifice the entire space program.

I'm not quite sure what I'm getting at,
as almost everything contradicts
but doesn't contradict everything,
as some truths are sacrificed to reveal others.
Said sacrifices are worthwhile,
others not so much.

Maybe you can't teach a robot how to sacrifice,
but a human can learn to sacrifice himself
to become one.

One Tier, Two Tier
Red Tear, Blue Tear

When girls cry, they do so
like a small child
that's just scraped their knee on the playground
or fallen down some stairs.
bawling, wailing,
tears streaming up?
and down their face
all over the place-
and with that quivering lip.

When I cry,
it's always a single tear
that draws a line and says so much
but more ambiguous
almost as if it were
a statue crying,
like the one from the end of "Battle for the Planet of the Apes".
Expressionless, inanimate,
one is left to wonder,
was it a tear for joy?
or one of sadness.

They Don't Understand

It's been said,
that some people can't leave things unsaid
of things they say we are
we do-
what cannot be undone.
They don't seem to understand,
walking and daydreaming go hand in hand.

Those pacing thoughts,
just wandering them on and off..
A nervous wreck in a messy room,
these are those in which progress depends,
where new systems are formed and others end.

At this epoch, an epic battle
between the conventional wisdom
of the unimaginative man
and the one who thinks he can-
and does,
fail and fail and try yet again.

In his view,
the weight of the world is on his shoulders.
They don't understand
the things we say we know, some of them
one day we actually will.
When Columbus sailed the ocean blue
they're the ones,
who said it couldn't be, and now would say
should not have been done.

They don't understand.

But you and I, I'm glad we're different.
We're a lot alike.
Before I found you,
I thought I was all alone
such a long time had passed
time I thought, time enough at last
like Harold Bemis in the twilight zone.

But now it seems finally I have someone
who sees the world the same as me
They'll never again be what once was.
From this day on, it's only we.
They don't understand,
it's just you and I who know the way
we see.
I'm glad you understand,
understand?
understand!
Oh, I see. It's just me.
It's okay,
I understand.

Perhaps only the phantom fathom can fathom the phantom.

In other words,
I guess I can understand you're inability to understand why
I don't understand why you don't understand how
I can't understand how you can't understand why
I won't understand why you don't understand why
I won't understand what I don't understand that
you understand and why you won't understand what
you don't understand that I understand.

Once more, once again;

They don't understand,
it's just you and I who know the way
we see.
I'm glad you understand,
understand?
understand!
Oh, I see. It's just me.
It's okay,
I understand.

www.brandonadamson.com